U.S.A. TRAVEL GUIDES

CALIFORNIA

BY ANN HEINRICHS • ILLUSTRATED BY MATT KANIA

The Child's World®
childsworld.com

Published by The Child's World®
1980 Lookout Drive • Mankato, MN 56003-1705
800-599-READ • www.childsworld.com

ISBN 9781503819450
LCCN 2016961122

Printing
Printed in the United States of America
PA02430

Ann Heinrichs is the author of more than 100 books for children and young adults. She has also enjoyed successful careers as a children's book editor and an advertising copywriter. Ann grew up in Fort Smith, Arkansas, and lives in Chicago, Illinois.

post card

About the Author
Ann Heinrichs

Matt Kania loves maps and, as a kid, dreamed of making them. In school he studied geography and cartography, and today he makes maps for a living. Matt's favorite thing about drawing maps is learning about the places they represent. Many of the maps he has created can be found in books, magazines, videos, Web sites, and public places.

post card

About the
Map Illustrator
Matt Kania

On the cover: Take in the views on Bixby Bridge along the Big Sur coast.

OUR CALIFORNIA TRIP

CALIFORNIA

Hey—let's check out the Golden State! Just follow the dotted line, or else skip around. Either way, you're in for a great ride. You'll meet Walt Disney and Charles Schulz. You'll visit gold mines, tar pits, and space labs. So buckle up that seat belt. We're on our way!

WELCOME TO CALIFORNIA

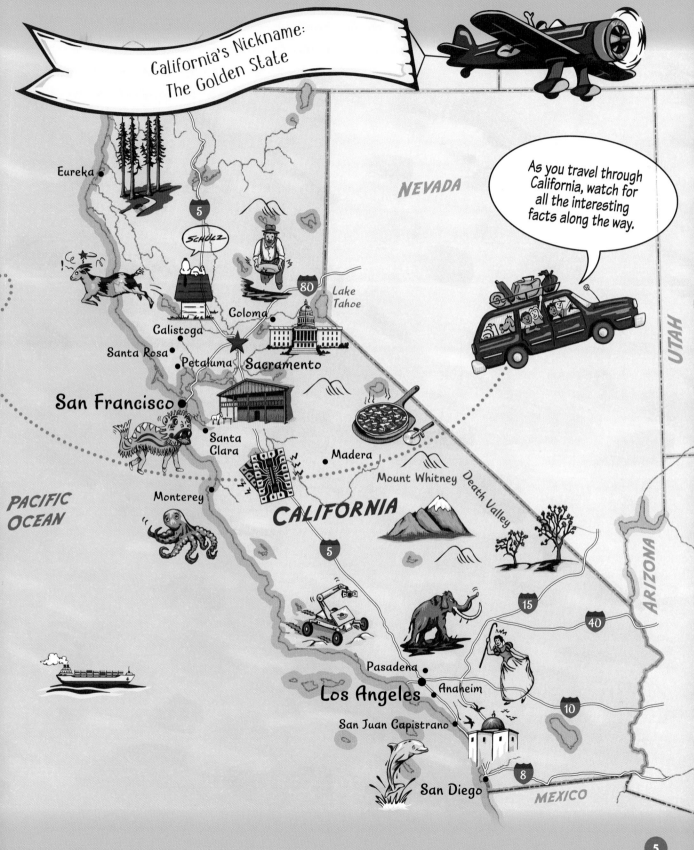

LA BREA TAR PITS

You'll find the La Brea Tar Pits in Los Angeles. It was a weird scene thousands of years ago. Tar bubbled up from deep underground. It formed pools of black, sticky goo. Thousands of animals got stuck in the tar. Later, scientists began finding their bones. They found wolves, bears, and mammoths. They even found lions, camels, and saber-toothed cats.

The tar was useful to Native Americans in the area. They used it as a glue. They also used it in making canoes and baskets. The tar made a tight seal. It kept water from seeping in.

A mammoth is stuck in the La Brea tar! Models show the animals that died there long ago.

THE SWALLOWS AT SAN JUAN CAPISTRANO

San Juan Capistrano is famous for its swallows. These little birds fly in every March to nest there. Thousands of people come to see them.

San Juan Capistrano is one of the California **missions**. They were the first European settlements in California. Spain ruled Mexico and California in the 1700s. Spanish people from Mexico moved into California. They built missions, forts, and villages. Many Spanish settlements became California cities.

Father Junípero Serra was a Catholic priest, or padre. He came from Mexico to build missions. He wanted to spread Christianity throughout California. Many Native Americans lived in the area. They had their own beliefs and customs. But the mission taught them Christianity instead. The Mission San Juan Capistrano was founded in 1776.

The Mission at San Juan Capistrano is now a museum.

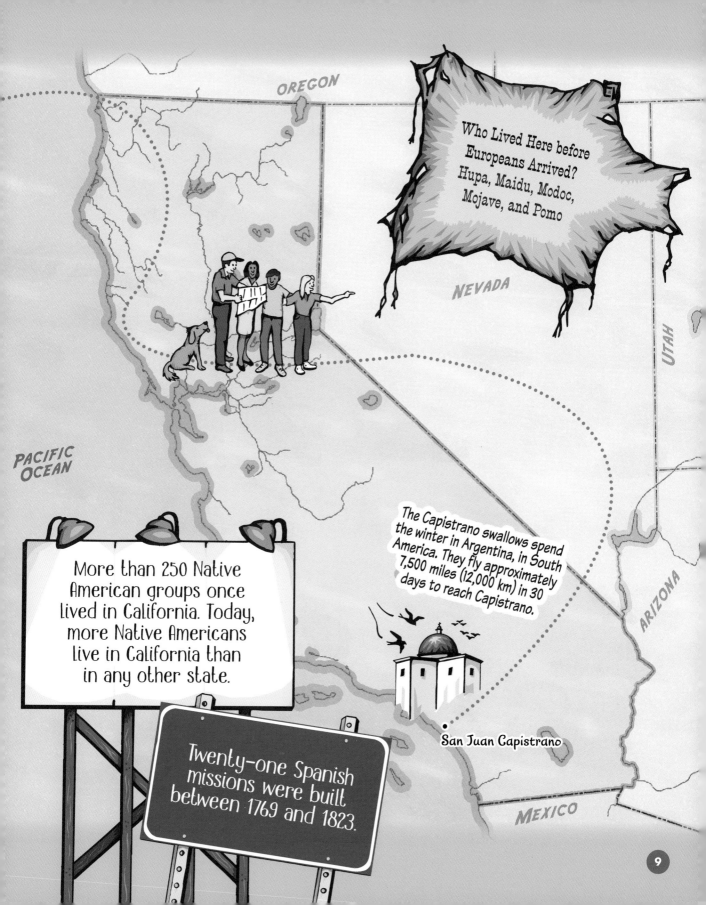

Who Lived Here before Europeans Arrived? Hupa, Maidu, Modoc, Mojave, and Pomo

More than 250 Native American groups once lived in California. Today, more Native Americans live in California than in any other state.

The Capistrano swallows spend the winter in Argentina, in South America. They fly approximately 7,500 miles (12,000 km) in 30 days to reach Capistrano.

San Juan Capistrano

Twenty-one Spanish missions were built between 1769 and 1823.

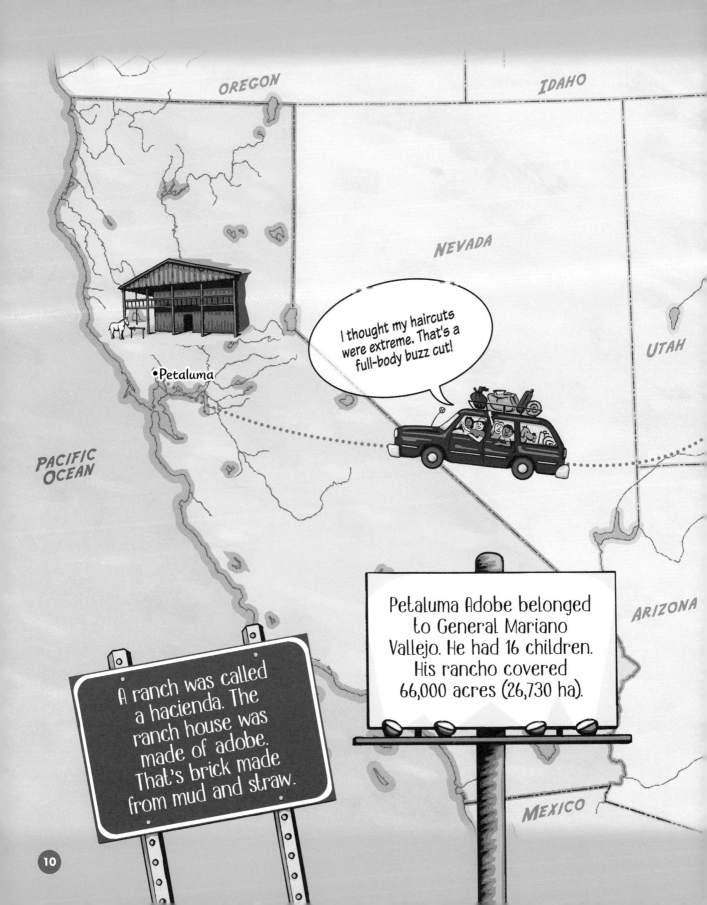

SHEEP SHEARING DAY AT PETALUMA ADOBE

Do you know how to shear a sheep? Here's how. First you hold the sheep. Then you start shaving it. So what's the hard part? Removing all the wool in one big piece!

Want to watch an expert do it? Just go to Sheep Shearing Day at Petaluma Adobe. That's when the sheep get their haircuts.

Petaluma Adobe was California's biggest ranch house. Hundreds of ranches covered California in the 1800s. How did the ranches begin? Mexico won freedom from Spain in 1821. Then Mexico ruled California. Mexico gave away most of the missions' land. It was divided into huge pieces of land called ranchos. The landowners were called rancheros. They grew rich raising cattle and sheep.

Baa! Is it time for a haircut at Petaluma Adobe? Don't worry, it doesn't hurt the sheep!

PANNING FOR GOLD AT SUTTER'S MILL

Want to find some gold? Just go to Sutter's Mill in Coloma. You can get a big old pan there. Then go down by the American River. Let the water flow into your pan. Do you see something sparkly? It's gold!

That's what James Marshall did in 1848. He was building a sawmill by the American River. One day he found gold in the river. His gold discovery started the California gold rush. By 1849, thousands of people were pouring in. They were called Forty-Niners. You can probably guess why!

New towns sprang up overnight. But people left if they didn't find gold. Some towns became ghost towns.

James Marshall spotted something shiny in the water… it was gold!

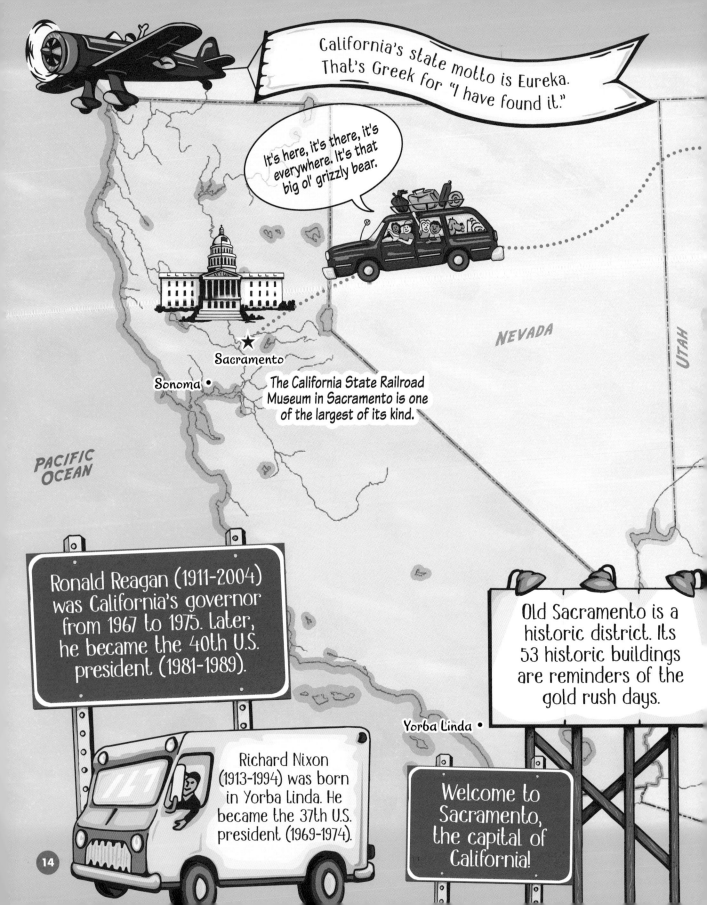

California's state motto is Eureka. That's Greek for "I have found it."

It's here, it's there, it's everywhere. It's that big ol' grizzly bear.

Sacramento

Sonoma

The California State Railroad Museum in Sacramento is one of the largest of its kind.

NEVADA

UTAH

PACIFIC OCEAN

Ronald Reagan (1911-2004) was California's governor from 1967 to 1975. Later, he became the 40th U.S. president (1981-1989).

Old Sacramento is a historic district. Its 53 historic buildings are reminders of the gold rush days.

Yorba Linda

Richard Nixon (1913-1994) was born in Yorba Linda. He became the 37th U.S. president (1969-1974).

Welcome to Sacramento, the capital of California!

THE BEAR FLAG AND THE STATE CAPITOL

The bear flag is California's state flag. The first bear flag showed up in 1846. American settlers in Sonoma made it. Now bear flags are everywhere in California. Just walk around inside the state capitol. They're hanging all over the place!

Many state government offices are in the capitol. California has three branches of government. One branch makes laws. Its members come from all over the state. The governor heads another branch. It carries out the laws. Courts make up the third branch. They decide whether someone has broken the law.

The state capitol is located in Sacramento. The building has been around since 1869!

PASADENA'S JET PROPULSION LABORATORY

What do Mars **rovers** do? They "shoot and scoot"! They take pictures and then they scoot somewhere else. Just tour the Jet Propulsion Laboratory in Pasadena. It makes **robot** spacecraft. You'll see how scientists make those rovers scoot! The Jet Propulsion Lab also includes the Space Flight Operations Facility. There, scientists gather data and keep track of astronauts up in space.

Space science is a big **industry** in California. America's space program did lots of testing there. Computer science became another hot industry. Many computer companies grew up in the Santa Clara Valley. Now that area is called Silicon Valley. Silicon is a material used in making **computer chips**.

The Space Flight Operations Facility monitors astronauts—maybe that could be you!

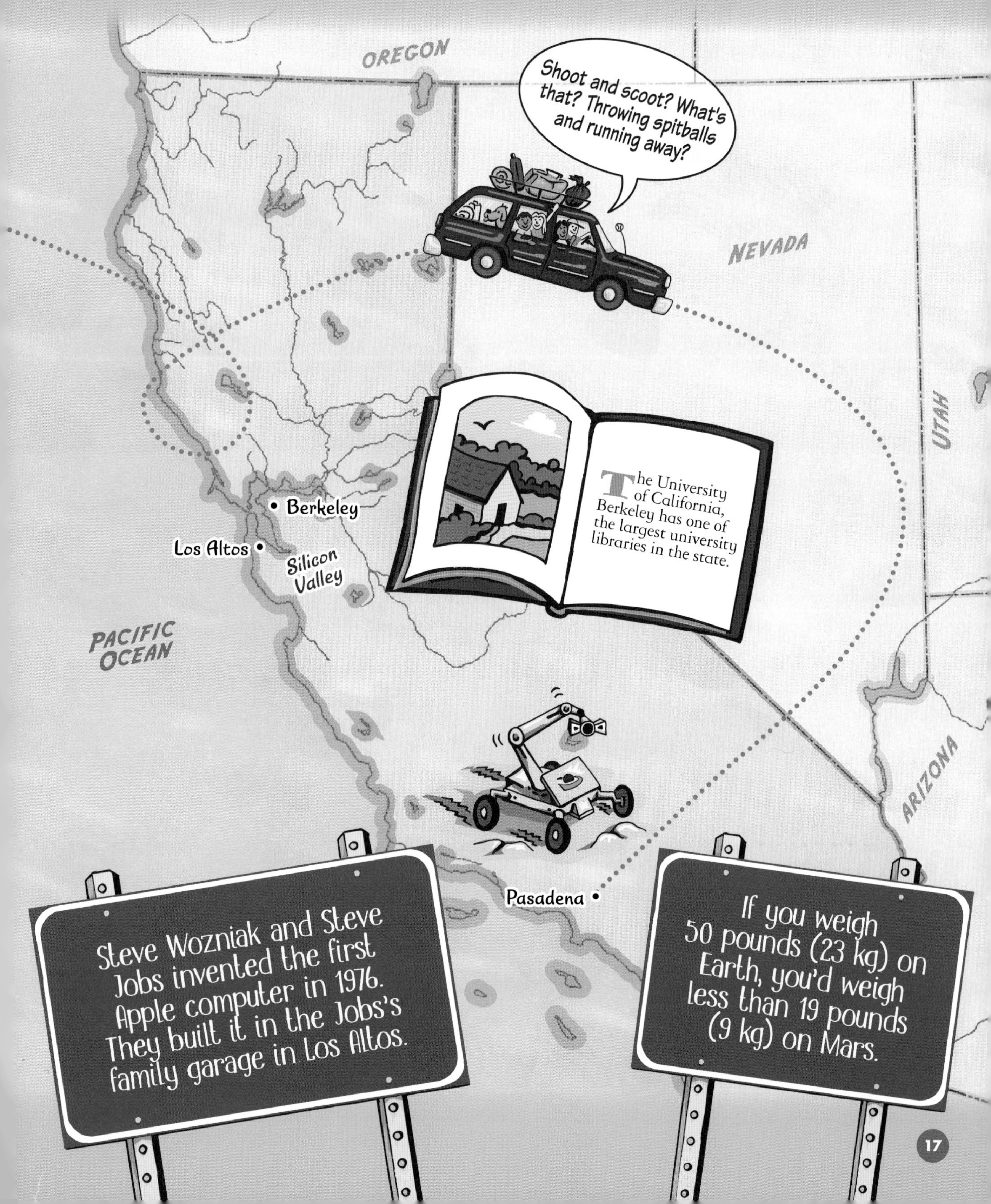

OREGON

NEVADA

UTAH

Shoot and scoot? What's that? Throwing spitballs and running away?

• Berkeley

Los Altos •

Silicon Valley

The University of California, Berkeley has one of the largest university libraries in the state.

PACIFIC OCEAN

ARIZONA

Pasadena •

Steve Wozniak and Steve Jobs invented the first Apple computer in 1976. They built it in the Jobs's family garage in Los Altos.

If you weigh 50 pounds (23 kg) on Earth, you'd weigh less than 19 pounds (9 kg) on Mars.

The Intel Museum is a fun place to visit. It's in Santa Clara. That's right in the heart of Silicon Valley.

Intel is the world's largest maker of computer chips. Its factory workers wear outfits called bunny suits! The suits keep the tiny computer parts clean. They keep people's hairs and skin flakes away. Kids love to visit Intel's museum. They get to try on bunny suits, too.

California makes more products than any other state. Computers and **electronics** are its major factory goods. Most are made in Silicon Valley.

Do you like computers? Then don't forget to visit the Intel Museum!

DEATH VALLEY, DESERTS, AND COASTS

Death Valley has a pretty scary name. But it's not all that deadly. Lots of animals and plants live there. If they can stand it, you can too!

Southeastern California is mostly deserts. One of them is Death Valley. Another is the Mojave Desert. Western California is much wetter. It faces the Pacific Ocean. The northern coast is often foggy and rainy. The southern coast is warm and sunny.

Two big mountain ranges run down California. The Coast Ranges rise near the coast. The other mountain range is the Sierra Nevada. It is located in eastern California. Between them is the Central Valley. It's a rich farming region.

Don't forget to bring water if you visit Death Valley! It's the hottest national park.

Lowest Temperature: Boca
January 20, 1937
-45°F (-43°C)

Highest Temperature: Greenland Ranch in Death Valley
July 10, 1913
134°F (57°C)

OREGON

NEVADA

Coast Ranges

Sacramento River

PACIFIC OCEAN

Central Valley

• Boca
• Blue Canyon

Sierra Nevada

• San Francisco

San Joaquin River

Coast Ranges

San Andreas Fault

Welcome to Death Valley? No thanks!

Mount Whitney

Death Valley has the hottest, driest, and lowest places in the country.

Death Valley

Mojave Desert

Greenland Ranch in Death Valley recorded the highest-ever U.S. temperature.

ARIZONA

Colorado River

California gets lots of earthquakes. San Francisco had a terrible earthquake in 1906.

California's major rivers are the Sacramento and the San Joaquin. Both flow through the Central Valley. The Colorado River forms the border between California and Arizona.

Blue Canyon is one of the snowiest cities in the country. It averages more than 250 inches (635 cm) of snow a year!

HIGHEST AND LOWEST POINTS
HIGHEST: Mount Whitney at 14,494 feet (4,418 m)
LOWEST: 282 feet (86 m) below sea level in Death Valley

STATE TREE:
CALIFORNIA REDWOOD

STATE FLOWER:
GOLDEN POPPY

STATE BIRD:
CALIFORNIA VALLEY QUAIL

The grizzly bear is California's state animal.

NEVADA

UTAH

Davis •

PACIFIC OCEAN

I spy a panda, I spy a hippo, I spy a giraffe. . .

What Are California's Fishing Products?
Squid, sea urchins, and crab

SeaWorld is home to nearly 13,000 animals.

ARIZO

San Diego •

California condors are the largest scavengers in North America.

The Frog Tunnel is at Toad Hollow in Davis. It was built so frogs could safely cross the road.

W hat is black and white and sleepy all over? Answer: a panda! Some live at the San Diego Zoo in southern California.

The San Diego Zoo is one of the world's biggest zoos. It's home to nearly 4,000 animals. Many of the animals are **endangered**, including the panda.

Plenty of sea critters live off California's coast. Crabs, lobsters, and dolphins are just a few. Foxes, jackrabbits, and mice live in the deserts. They scurry around cactuses and other tough plants. Bighorn sheep prance up in the mountains. You'll be lucky to see bighorn sheep, though. Typically they are wary of humans.

The San Diego Zoo's pandas eat more than 700 pounds (317 kg) of bamboo each week. That's a lot of bamboo!

CALISTOGA AND THE FAINTING GOATS

Boo! That's all it takes. Kerplunk! The goat's on the ground. It's stiff as a board. It must be a fainting goat!

Some California farmers raise fainting goats. Surprise one, and it gets stiff and falls over. Fainting goats have a disorder called myotonia congenita. They don't really faint. They're wide awake when they fall.

Tourists come to see the fainting goats of Calistoga. But it takes a lot to scare them now. They're bored with people saying "Boo!"

When fainting goats panic, their muscles seize up for three seconds.

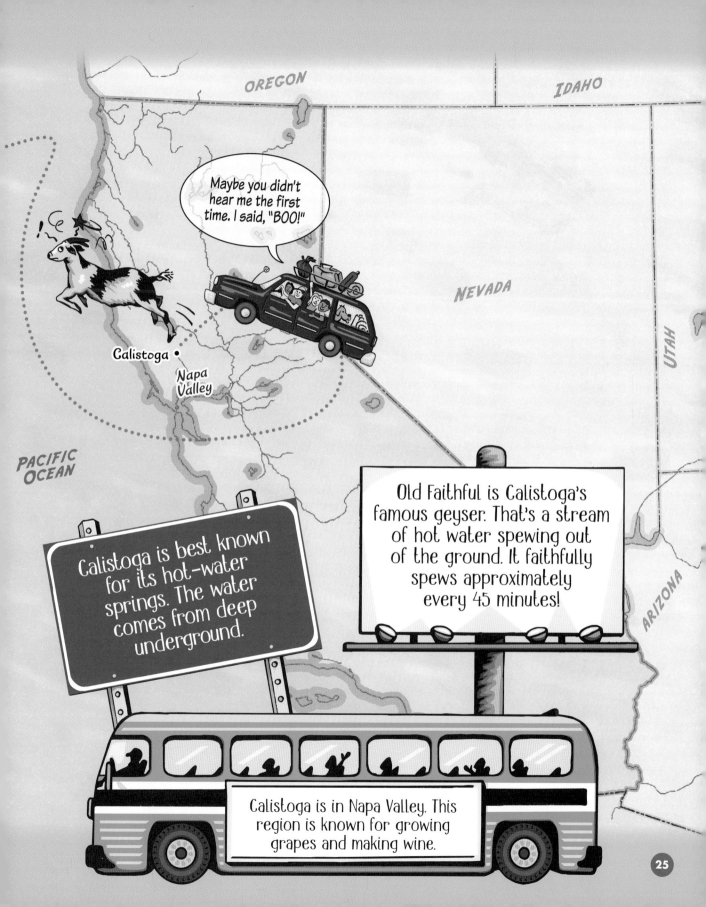

THE GIANT REDWOODS

You're driving along the Avenue of the Giants. It runs near California's north coast, near Eureka. You take a turn into the forest. All of a sudden, you're in a dark tunnel. You're driving right through a giant tree trunk!

California's redwood trees are huge. They are the world's tallest living things. People have cut tunnels through some redwoods' trunks. The result? Drive through trees!

Redwoods once grew in the **Petrified** Forest, too. They lived more than three million years ago. Now they have turned to stone!

Want to see the oldest, tallest trees around? Take a drive down the Avenue of the Giants.

MADERA'S PIZZA FARM

Check out the pizza farm in Madera. It grows all the things that go into pizza. The farm is even shaped like a pizza! Each "slice" grows a different ingredient. There's wheat for the crust. There's dairy cattle for the cheese. There's tomatoes, peppers, and herbs. Is your mouth watering yet?

California is the nation's leading farm state. Some of the biggest farms are in the Central Valley. That's where the pizza farm is. The Imperial Valley in the south has lots of farms, too.

Fruits, nuts, and vegetables are important crops. Many farmers raise milk and beef cattle. Some raise sheep or chickens, too.

Can't have pizza without tomatoes! The pizza farm in Madera grows all the ingredients needed to make pizza.

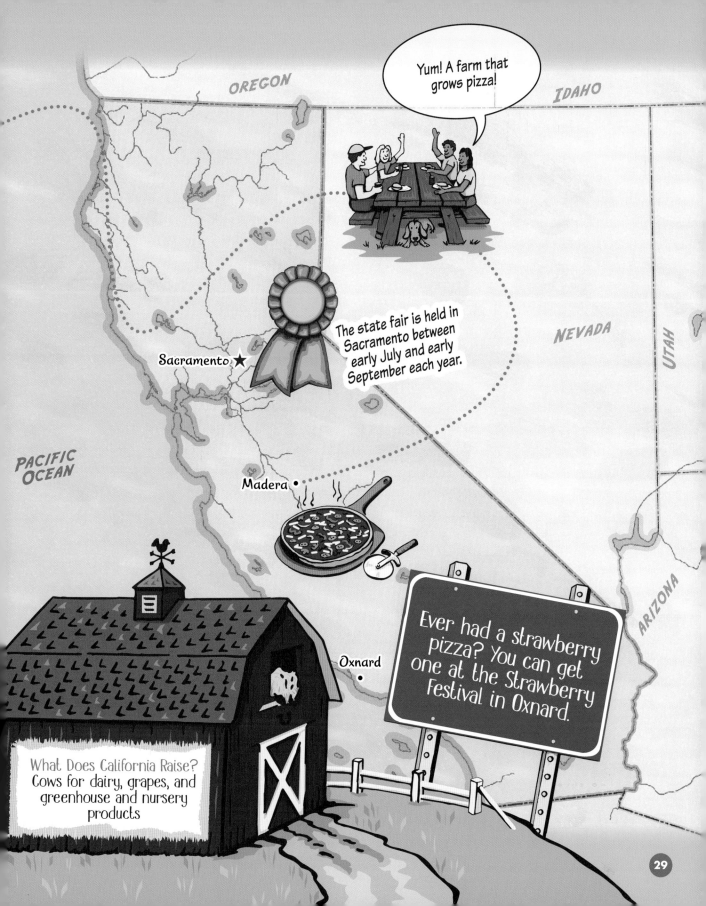

THE CHARLES M. SCHULZ MUSEUM

Santa Rosa had a famous resident—Charles M. Schulz. Schulz created the *Peanuts* comic strip. He thought up Snoopy, Charlie Brown, and Lucy. He invented Schroeder, Linus, and Peppermint Patty, too. Do you have a favorite *Peanuts* character?

The Charles M. Schulz Museum is fun to visit. It's full of *Peanuts* art. It also has a nice, cozy theater. There you can curl up and watch *Peanuts* cartoons. They run for hours!

Who's your favorite Peanuts *character? Visit them all at the Charles M. Schulz Museum.*

Blast into space. Sail down a jungle river. Visit a fairy castle. Meet pirates, ghosts, and flying elephants. It could only happen in Disneyland!

Walt Disney invented Mickey Mouse in 1928. He made hundreds of cartoons and movies. But he wanted to create even more fun for kids. So he opened Disneyland in Anaheim.

Anaheim is close to Hollywood. That's the moviemaking capital of the world. Lots of television shows are made there, too.

Want to see Sleeping Beauty's castle? You can at Disneyland!

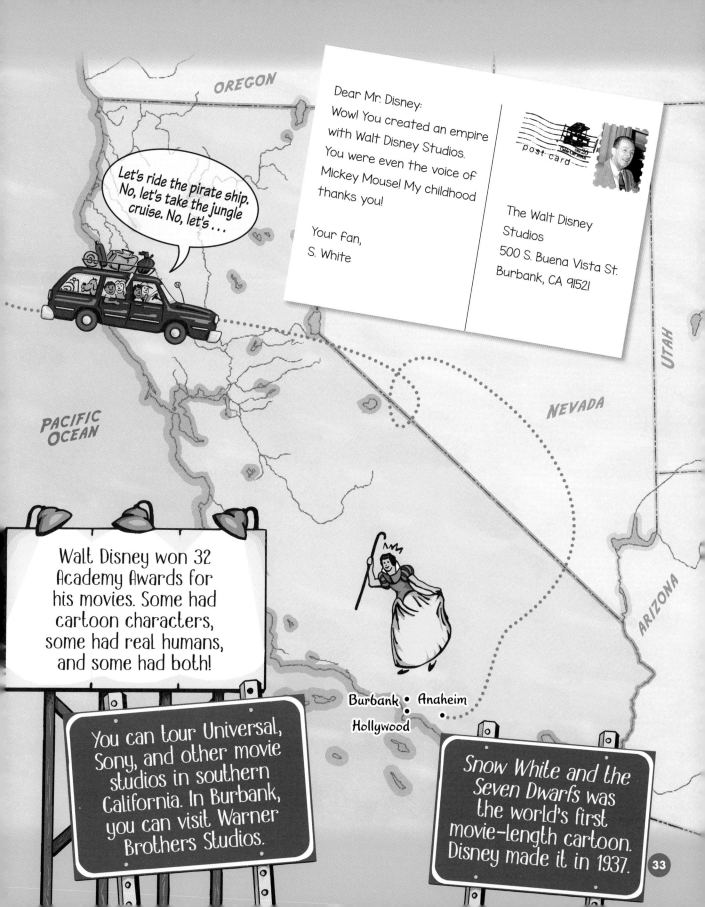

Let's ride the pirate ship. No, let's take the jungle cruise. No, let's ...

Dear Mr. Disney:
Wow! You created an empire with Walt Disney Studios. You were even the voice of Mickey Mouse! My childhood thanks you!

Your fan,
S. White

post card

The Walt Disney Studios
500 S. Buena Vista St.
Burbank, CA 91521

OREGON

PACIFIC OCEAN

NEVADA

UTAH

ARIZONA

Walt Disney won 32 Academy Awards for his movies. Some had cartoon characters, some had real humans, and some had both!

Burbank • Anaheim
Hollywood

You can tour Universal, Sony, and other movie studios in southern California. In Burbank, you can visit Warner Brothers Studios.

Snow White and the Seven Dwarfs was the world's first movie-length cartoon. Disney made it in 1937.

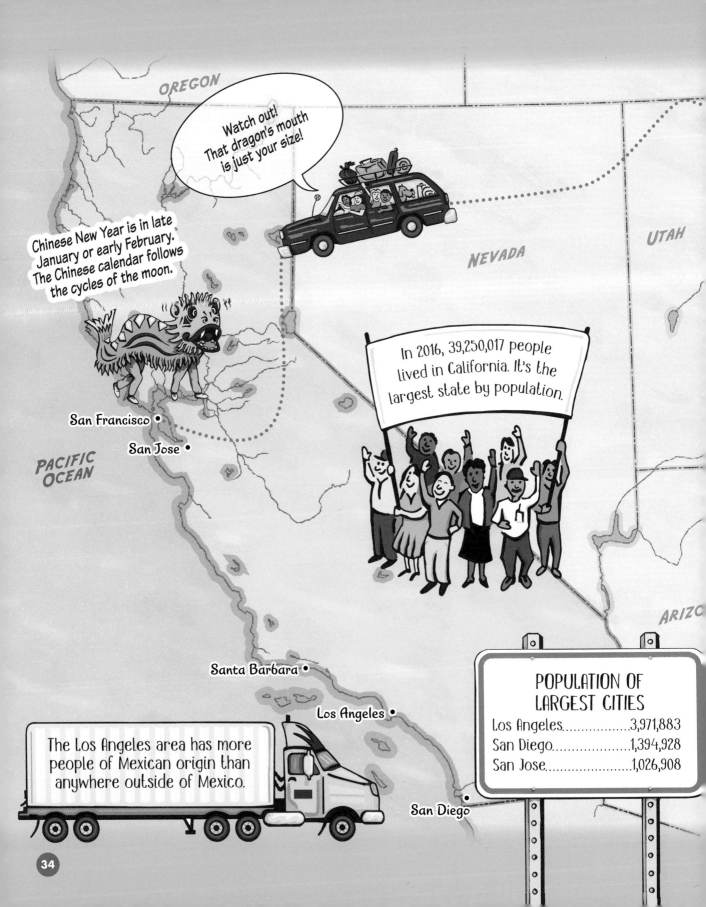

OREGON

Watch out! That dragon's mouth is just your size!

Chinese New Year is in late January or early February. The Chinese calendar follows the cycles of the moon.

NEVADA

UTAH

In 2016, 39,250,017 people lived in California. It's the largest state by population.

San Francisco •

San Jose •

PACIFIC OCEAN

ARIZO

Santa Barbara •

Los Angeles •

The Los Angeles area has more people of Mexican origin than anywhere outside of Mexico.

POPULATION OF LARGEST CITIES

Los Angeles..................3,971,883
San Diego...................1,394,928
San Jose.....................1,026,908

San Diego •

Firecrackers are popping! Dragons are dancing down the street! It's Chinese New Year in San Francisco!

Many Chinese **immigrants** settled in San Francisco. They built up the Chinatown area. It's one of the biggest Chinese neighborhoods outside of Asia.

Many Hispanic, or Latino, people also live in California. Most have Mexican roots. Hispanic festivals are colorful and exciting. One is the Old Spanish Days Fiesta in Santa Barbara.

Dozens of other **ethnic** groups live in California. Each group has special foods and customs. Want to see the world? Just visit California!

The San Francisco Chinese New Year is the largest new year celebration in North America.

OUR TRIP

We visited many amazing places on our trip! We also met a lot of interesting people along the way. Look at the map below. Use your finger to trace all the places we have been.

Do you remember what California's state fossil is? *See page 6 for the answer.*

How many children did General Mariano Vallejo have? *Page 10 has the answer.*

Which U.S. president was born in California? *See page 14 for the answer.*

What tasty candies can you sample in Fairfield? *Look on page 18 for the answer.*

How many animals live at SeaWorld? *Page 22 has the answer.*

Where can you get a strawberry pizza? *Turn to page 29 for the answer.*

What kind of drawing pen did Charles Schulz have? *Look on page 30 and find out!*

How many Academy Awards did Walt Disney win? *Turn to page 33 for the answer.*

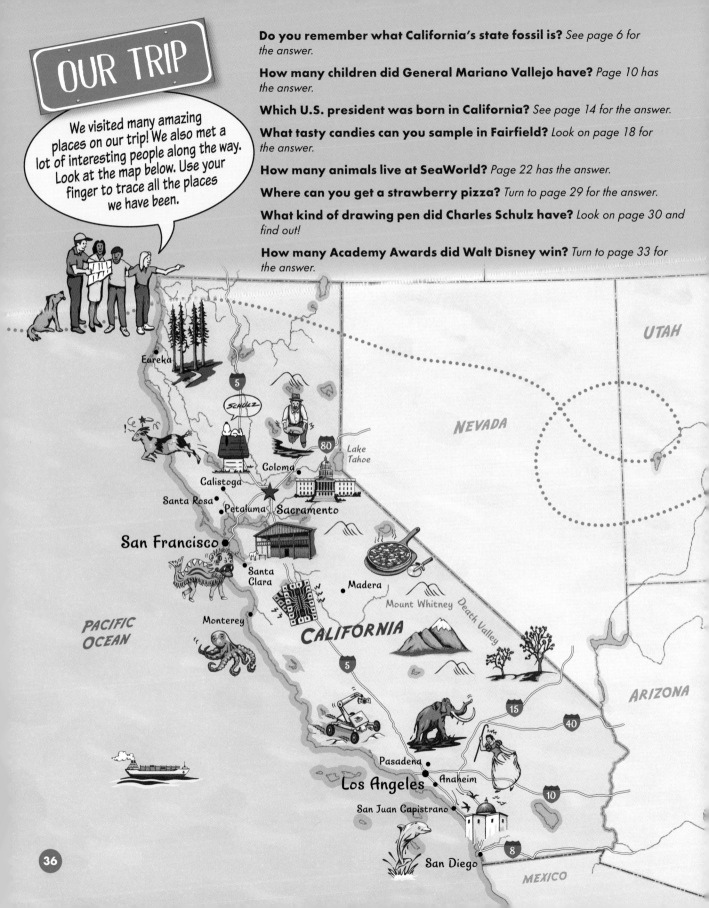

UTAH

NEVADA

Eureka

Schulz

Lake Tahoe

Coloma

Calistoga

Santa Rosa

Petaluma

Sacramento

San Francisco

Santa Clara

Madera

Mount Whitney

Death Valley

CALIFORNIA

PACIFIC OCEAN

Monterey

ARIZONA

Pasadena

Los Angeles

Anaheim

San Juan Capistrano

San Diego

MEXICO

STATE SYMBOLS

State animal: California grizzly bear

State bird: California valley quail

State fish: California golden trout

State flower: California poppy (golden poppy)

State fossil: Saber-toothed cat

State gemstone: Blue diamond (benitoite)

State insect: California dogface butterfly

State marine fish: Garibaldi

State marine mammal: Gray whale

State mineral: Gold

State reptile: Desert tortoise

State rock: Serpentine

State soil: San Joaquin soil

State tree: California redwood

State seal

STATE SONG

"I LOVE YOU, CALIFORNIA"
Words by F. B. Silverwood, music by A. F. Frankenstein

I love you, California, you're the greatest state of all.
I love you in the winter, summer, spring and in the fall.
I love your fertile valleys, your dear mountains I adore.
I love your grand old ocean and I love her rugged shore.

Chorus:
Where the snow-crowned Golden Sierras
Keep their watch o'er the valleys' bloom,
It is there I would be in our land by the sea,
Ev'ry breeze bearing rich perfume.
It is here nature gives of her rarest. It is Home Sweet Home to me,
And I know when I die I shall breathe my last sigh
For my sunny California.

I love your redwood forests—love your fields of yellow grain.
I love your summer breezes and I love your winter rain.
I love you, land of flowers; land of honey, fruit and wine.
I love you, California; you have won this heart of mine.

I love your old gray Missions, love your vineyards stretching far.
I love you, California, with your Golden Gate ajar.
I love your purple sunsets, love your skies of azure blue.
I love you, California; I just can't help loving you.

I love you, Catalina, you are very dear to me;
I love you, Tamalpais, and I love Yosemite;
I love you, land of sunshine, half your beauties are untold;
I loved you in my childhood, and I'll love you when I'm old.

That was a great trip! We have traveled all over California! There were a few places that we didn't have time for, though. Next time, we plan to visit the Monterey Bay Aquarium. There are approximately 550 different types of plants and animals on display! That number includes penguins, otters, sharks, turtles, and whales.

State flag

FAMOUS PEOPLE

Anniston, Jennifer (1969–), film and television actress

Chávez, César (1927–1993), labor leader

Child, Julia (1912–2004), world-famous chef

Cleary, Beverly (1916–), children's author

DiMaggio, Joe (1914–1999), baseball legend

Disney, Walt (1901–1966), film producer, animator

Garcia, Jerry (1942–1995), singer with the Grateful Dead

Ishi (ca. 1862–1916), the last of the Yahi people

Jobs, Steve (1955–2011) inventor

Johnson, Earvin "Magic" (1959–), former basketball player

Johnson, Jimmie (1975–), NASCAR racer

Lamar, Kendrick (1987–), rapper and songwriter

Lucas, George (1944–), film director and producer

Marshall, James (1810–1885), gold miner

Monroe, Marilyn (1926–1962), movie star

Nixon, Richard (1913–1994), 37th U.S. president

Perry, Katy (1984–), singer and songwriter

Reagan, Ronald (1911–2004), 40th U.S. president

Ride, Sally K. (1951–2012), 1st American woman astronaut

Ryan, Pam Muñoz (1951–), children's author

Say, Allen (1937–), children's author

Schwarzenegger, Arnold (1947–), movie star and former governor of California

Valens, Ritchie (1941–1959), legendary rock 'n' roll singer

Woods, Eldrick "Tiger" (1975–), champion golfer

WORDS TO KNOW

computer chips (kuhm-PYOO-tur CHIPS) very small computer parts that make the computer work

electronics (i-lek-TRON-iks) a science that deals with tiny particles called electrons

endangered (en-DAYN-jurd) When a species or plant is in danger of no longer existing

ethnic (ETH-nik) relating to a person's race or nation

fossil (FOSS-uhl) a bone or print of something that lived on Earth long ago

Ice Age (EYESS AJE) a time when the world was covered in ice

immigrants (IM-uh-gruhnts) people who move from their home country to another country

industry (IN-duh-stree) a type of business

missions (MISH-uhnz) religious centers devoted to spreading a faith

petrified (PET-ruh-fide) turned into stone

robot (ROH-bot) a machine that can do human tasks

rovers (ROH-vurz) people or things that shift from place to place

TO LEARN MORE

IN THE LIBRARY

Duffield, Katy S. *California History for Kids: Missions, Miners, and Moviemakers in the Golden State.* Chicago, IL: Chicago Review Press, 2012.

Friedman, Mel. *The California Gold Rush.* New York, NY: Scholastic, Inc., 2010.

Gendell, Megan. *The Spanish Missions of California.* New York, NY: Scholastic, Inc., 2010.

ON THE WEB

Visit our Web site for links about California:

childsworld.com/links

Note to Parents, Teachers, and Librarians: We routinely verify our Web links to make sure they are safe and active sites. So encourage your readers to check them out!

PLACES TO VISIT OR CONTACT

California Historical Society

californiahistoricalsociety.org

678 Mission Street

San Francisco, CA 94105

415/357-1848

For more information about the history of California

California Tourism

visitcalifornia.com

555 Capitol Mall Suite 1100

Sacramento, CA 95814

877/225-4367

For more information about visiting California

California covers 163,696 square miles (423,971 sq km). It's the 3rd-largest state in size.

INDEX

Bye, Golden State. We had a great time. We'll come back soon!